UNSOLVED MYSTERIES
OF THE
COPPER COUNTRY

The Case of George C Sheldon

P. GERMAIN

authorHOUSE®

AuthorHouse™
1663 Liberty Drive
Bloomington, IN 47403
www.authorhouse.com
Phone: 1-800-839-8640

First published by AuthorHouse 11/21/2009

ISBN: 978-1-4389-9639-4 (sc)

Printed in the United States of America
Bloomington, Indiana

This book is printed on acid-free paper.

Beloved is one of my favorite words.
I use it to describe my grandchildren.
This unsolved mystery is dedicated to my beloved granddaughters,
Abi and Caiti Bair, doll face and angel face respectively.

George Shelden also used this same favorite word of mine to
describe his grandchildren when he gave, devised, and bequeathed
his estate to his beloved grandchildren.
May each of you use the word, beloved, to describe a person in
your own life!

Contents

Author's Note

The Copper Country's greatest strength is that families continue to reside here, generation after generation. That is why I have always felt cosseted and protected from the outside world. Grandparents, parents, and children are friends. Because of these long-term friendships, people can recount a family's trials and triumphs on a moment's notice. It is a comfortable niche in the world far from the madding crowd.

I have a reverence for the people of the past. To them, I owe a debt of gratitude, as I thank my God of History for choosing me as His writing instrument.

Some of our pioneering people were larger than life in life and remain so in death. George C. Shelden is one of them.

As I Remain

P. Germain
712 Pine Street
Calumet, MI 49913
Telephone: 1-906-337-3854

Unsolved Mysteries of the Copper Country, No. 2, the story of George C. Shelden, began when I noted that all over the city and county are reminders of the Shelden family's impact on the area. Shelden Avenue is the main street in the City of Houghton, and the Shelden Center is one of the beautiful sandstone buildings in the heart of the city. Before I knew it, my fascination with the Shelden family gave birth to the second in a series of unsolved mysteries. This story can be read as a stand-alone story or as part of the Unsolved Mysteries of the Copper Country series. It is my fervent hope that you will become enmeshed in the story of the area and the people who made the Copper Country what it is. I remain fierce in preserving the truth without causing anyone anguish by the story telling.

As I started reading and getting to know the historic Houghton families, Shelden, Shields, Edwards, Rice, Hubbell, and Houghton; their names were often coupled with Wright, Cox, Rees, Goodell, and Gundlach. This story began when Therissa Houghton married Ransom Shelden. Their union not only united two illustrious families, but also joined two separate fortunes. Instead of each family working against each other, by sharing their business strategies, they both were able to thrive in all their business ventures so that everything they touched turned to gold . . . silver . . . and copper in their pockets.

Ransom Shelden, George Shelden's father, had once owned all the property within the Village of Houghton and built the first building within the Village limits. His legacy was great and instilled in his children a desire to gain their father's approval by achieving success on their own. All the Sheldens loved their God, their families, and the financial empires they built.

George Shelden and his family lived on Montezuma Street in Houghton. His brother, Carlos, lived right next door. Both homes had a panoramic view of the Portage Lift Bridge which connected the twin cities of Houghton and Hancock. On Sundays, the Shelden family attended worship services at the Trinity Episcopal Church and was one of the founding families of the church. Their house and God's house were both on the same street.

His workplace at 602 Shelden Avenue was only a few blocks away from his home. While Ransom envisioned a bustling community with plenty of commerce, he spearheaded dredging a channel so that boats could come right into Houghton, and the town would grow. He was a speculator in real estate and mining ventures, also. George had his own vision. He envisioned a building of the finest materials and workmanship to house men of great business acumen. The signage in the Cyberia Cafe window states that George purchased this corner lot for $8,500 in 1889. Then he solicited investors to finance the building and bring his dream into fruition right in the hub of Houghton. George planned to use red sandstone quarried locally to build his dream, and he thought that the only thing wrong with the American dream was that there were too few dreamers left.

For the present year, 1896, George could even look across the street and see his father's grand historic home as he worked. It was hard to believe that his father had been gone 18 years already. He could see in his mind's eye the building he would establish which would stand on the north side of Shelden Avenue next to the bank with only Isle Royale Street separating the two buildings. It would become an icon of commerce. At night, he and his wife, Mary, refined the building plans and decided to adhere to the classic revival style with massive, grand doors and the new prismatic glass that Frank Lloyd Wright had patented bringing light into the deep recesses of the building. Little did Frank Lloyd Wright know that he would soon meet a woman who would become his mistress and have to deal with her murder, the murder of her two children, and four others.

George Shelden was a member of the Onigaming Yacht Club which was a private club for affluent residents. George liked the exclusivity of the Club. He liked it so much that he had a cemetery designed for the Shelden family, so that even in death he and his family would be insulated from those of a lesser station in life.

From his club and his church, to his workplace and his home, all the buildings he frequented were less than three miles apart. On a daily basis, he need go only a few blocks from his home to his offices in the Village of Houghton.

On the following page is a map of the bustling Village, now a city. The listing of the key buildings in this story and the photograph of the Shelden home, a veritable mansion, will orient you to the setting of the events which took place in the Fall of 1896.

As I perused the maps of the City of Houghton, I found the Shelden-Douglass Addition to the City, then the Shelden-Columbian Addition, and also the Hubbell Addition with street names of Blanche, Florence, and Hubbell Avenue. How powerful these men must have been to name the streets after themselves and their family members.

It is notable that Florence Avenue no longer exists. That particular street is Houghton Avenue today. I do hope that the name wasn't changed while Florence Hubbell was still alive. Dakota Street has also been renamed Bridge Street.

Shelden Avenue, Montezuma Avenue, Dakota Street (now Bridge Street), the Portage Lift Bridge, and the distances to the club and cemetery were in close proximity. All the people and places that George held most dear were within a three-mile loop.

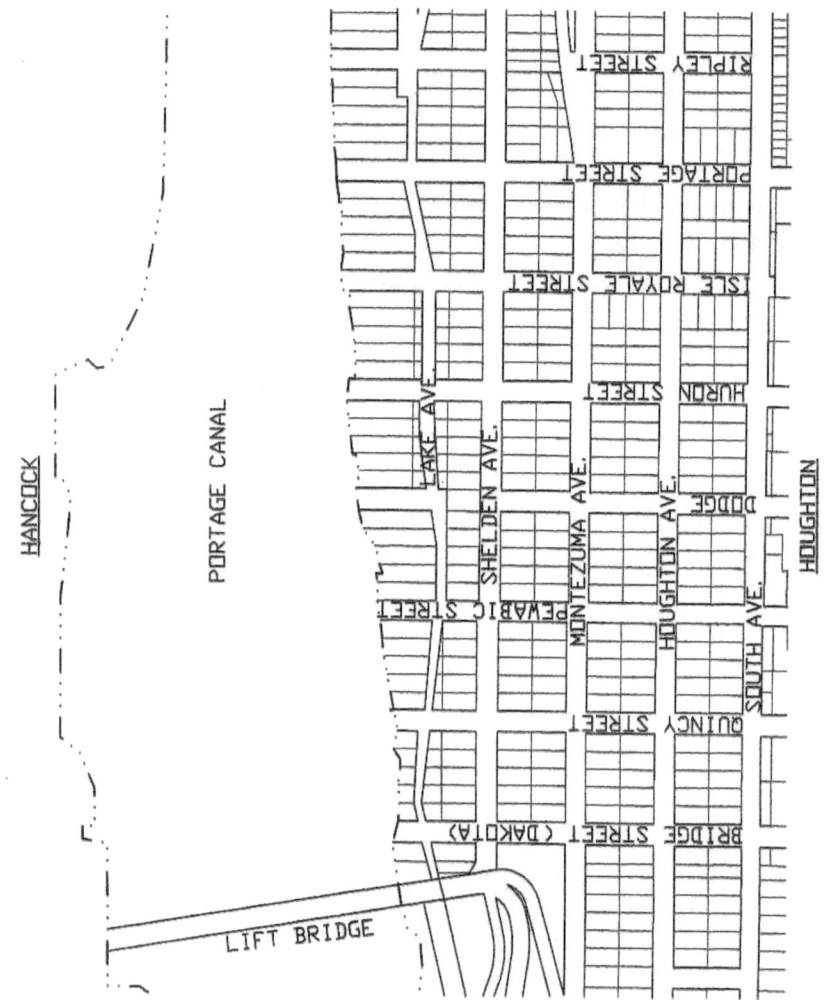

Map credit: U. P. Engineers & Architects, Inc.

Key Buildings

Carlos D. Shelden residence south side Montezuma 3 west of Dakota (Bridge)
Forest Hill Cemetery
Portage twp. south side Main
3/4 mile east of Franklin
George C. Shelden residence south side Montezuma 2 west of Dakota (Bridge)
Krellwitz's Undertaking Rooms north side Montezuma 1 west of Huron
Onigaming Yacht Club
3 miles southeast of Houghton
George's brother, Carlos, was the commander of the club.
Portage Lake Mining Gazette northeast corner Shelden and Portage
Post Office west side Isle Royale 3 north of Shelden
Shelden Block northwest corner Shelden and Isle Royale
R. Skiff had offices in the Shelden Block.
He was an esquire.
Shelden Private Cemetery
Portage twp, south side Main
3/4 mile east of Franklin
Trinity Episcopal Church southwest corner Pewabic and Montezuma

The Shelden home was one of the impressive Houghton mansions. If George's home was not the crown jewel of Houghton, it certainly housed one of the royal families.

Located at the top of a hill, the Shelden home was nestled in a lovely park-like setting where often there was a game of croquet on the lawn. In the Fall of 1896, the trees were just beginning to change color. By the first week of October, the village of Hancock on the hill across the lake would be cloaked in greens, yellows, golds, oranges, and brilliant russets.

Even though George was born in December, his favorite time of the year was the Fall. George loved orchestrating real estate deals, and he felt the pride which comes from hard work. He derived so much satisfaction from his work that every time he locked his office, George knew that he could never willingly face retirement.

Photo credit: MTU Archives and Copper Country Historical Collections, Michigan Technological University.

Before you continue to read the story, look at the microfilm copy on page 9. Then view the enlargement on the page after that. While the larger copy is easier to read, neither is as user-friendly as the original newspaper once was.

In order to read an entire page, you view the shrunken image. If you attempt to print it out, though, the print is too small to read. By turning the central lever from left to right, you get a blown-up copy but need to print several copies as you are only doing a small portion at a time at 30 cents a copy.

After a few hours of squinting to read the copy, scrolling forward, and fast-forwarding into reverse, I decided that microfilm may be a good storage method, but only if you don't wish to retrieve the data. It doesn't matter to me if 999 out of 1,000 pages are perfect, if the 1,000th page is the one I wish to view and it is indecipherable, I would not wish to rely on microfilm. I would make it illegal to save information on microfilm if there would ever be a need to retrieve it.

You may wish to take Dramamine for the symptoms you experience after using a microfilm reader. This is known as Researcher's Disease, and it is akin to seasickness.

See for yourself!

Microfilm Copy Credit: MTU Archives and Copper Country Historical Collections, Michigan Technological University.

Enlarged Microfilm Copy Credit: MTU Archives and Copper Country Historical Collections, Michigan Technological University.

Now that you have seen how difficult microfilm copies are to read, you will have a better understanding of how time consuming, frustrating, and expensive data retrieval can be. That is why for your reading pleasure and to prevent eyestrain, I have rekeyed all the microfilm copies so you can concentrate on the story.

The following newspaper articles appeared in the local newspapers of the day. The newspaper articles provide a chronological accounting of the George C. Shelden case. While the readership may have found the story to be front-page news, the Shelden story was relegated to the inside pages in the Shelden's hometown of Houghton. Because L'Anse was far enough away so as not to be unduly impacted by offending one of the most prominent families, it is notable that all the articles appeared on pages three or four in Houghton, but in L'Anse, 25 miles away, the articles commanded front-page coverage.

As you read the story of a man who was as rich as Croesus born into the coveted Copper Country haute monde, you will see that he had every gift except that of long life.

CALENDARS

September 1896

Sunday	Monday	Tuesday	Wednesday	Thursday	Friday	Saturday
		1	2	3	4	5
6	7	8	9	10	11	12
13	14	15	16	17	18	19
20	21	22	23	24	25	26
27	28	29	30			

October 1896

Sunday	Monday	Tuesday	Wednesday	Thursday	Friday	Saturday
				1	2	3
4	5	6	7	8	9	10
11	12	13	14	15	16	17
18	19	20	21	22	23	24
25	26	27	28	29	30	31

Article 1
The Portage Lake Mining Gazette
VOL. XXXVIII., NO, 11.--WHOLE NO 1975
September 17, 1896
Page 3
DEATH BY SUICIDE

Ira J. Whitney Shoots Himself in Forest Hill Cemetery, Houghton.

Last Friday afternoon, great excitement prevailed in Houghton when it was reported that Ira J. Whitney, traveling salesman for Smith, Wallace & Company, of Chicago, wholesale boot and shoe manufacturers, had committed suicide at Forest Hill cemetery. He had transacted business with his firm's customers as usual, and according to his order book the last sale was made to Peter Ruppe & Son, of Hancock, on Thursday evening. Friday morning he purchased a revolver from Pinton's Hardware store, in Hancock. He next came over to Houghton where he procured a small box from Matt Haug and placed his large diamond shirt stud and other jewelry in it and expressed it to his wife at Green Bay. After doing this he wrote six letters and handed them to Postmaster Dube, and remarked that "It was a beautiful day." He then went to a barber shop and got a shave. From there he made his way to the cemetery. There he met Charles Baudin, the sexton, and remarked that it was warm and taking off his hat at the same time wiped his brow with his handkerchief. Mr. Baudin did not notice anything strange about the visitor and he went in one direction and Whitney in another. Soon Baudin heard three reports from a pistol and going in the direction from which the sound came he found the man lying on his face with two bullet holes in his left side and another in his right ear. Information was immediately carried to Justice Brand who with Marshal Foley and a coroner's jury consisting of W. J. Vivian, J. B. Pfeiffer, M. J. Sullivan, W. T. Hooper, John Strobel and Matt Haug viewed the remains and rendered the following verdict: "We, the jury, find from the evidence that the deceased came to his death by his own hand." The remains were then taken to Undertaker Krellwitz's establishment where they were made ready to be forwarded to Green Bay. Mr. R. M. Hoar telegraphed Smith, Wallace & Co. what had happened and asked what should be done with the remains. A reply was received by Mr. Hoar that he should telegraph Mr. Whitney's wife at Green Bay which he did and received a reply that one of the firm from the Chicago base would come to Houghton. Accordingly Saturday noon's train brought Mr. Smith and a Mr. Crane. The latter will hereafter look after the firm's business in the Copper Country and take on where Mr. Whitney left off. Mr. Smith and Mr. Geo. C. Shelden left on the 2:25 train for Green Bay with the remains.

The deceased had traveled through the copper region for the past thirty-three years, and with the exception of one trip, he had always sold in the interest of boot and shoe houses. We learn from Mr. R. M. Hoar that he bought a bill of goods from him in September, 1863. This was Mr. Whitney's first trip to this region and he was then connected with Benedict, Hall & Co., of New York. He was then about 24 years of age and was counted the second largest salesman on the road. Through his pleasant, courteous manner and business tact, he won an enviable reputation. After three years of valuable service for this firm he started in business for himself with two other gentlemen. The firm did business under the title of Whitney, Cook & Co., at Broadway, New York. Finally after three years more this firm failed and Mr. Whitney went to Chicago, where he entered the employ of Greensfelder, Rosenthal & Co. and succeeded John Telling. Since then, however, he has traveled for several firms out of that city.

He was born in 1839 at North Adams, Mass., where he lived through his boyhood days. He was well educated and a man of refinement and could speak the German and Spanish languages. He was a member of the Masonic Lodge in Boston and a charter member of the Lotus Club of New York City. A widow and three children survive him.

★★★★★

George Shelden may have accompanied the body, because he had been retained by Ira Whitby to prepare Ira's Last Will and Testament. It could have been necessary for him to read and record the will and discuss the voided insurance policies with Ira's widow. He may have merely been a friend and wanted to offer the family his condolences.

Regardless of his reason for traveling to Green Bay with Mr. Smith, it was a sad journey for the pair.

George disdained of publicity and could never imagine suicide as an option. He believed that suicide was a permanent solution for a temporary problem. He thought that only weak men killed themselves. Little would he know that his strength would be the cause of his own demise and that in little more than a fortnight he, too, would be dead.

Article 2
Portage Lake Mining Gazette
Vol. XXXVIII., NO, 12.--WHOLE NO 1976
September 24, 1896
Page 3

ABOUT PORTAGE LAKE.

Monday afternoon as Mr. George C. Shelden was driving his pair of horses across the bridge, from the Houghton to the Hancock side, he was crowded several times by a man by the name of Chas. Hanson, of Atlantic Mine, who was driving a single rig in the same direction. As soon as Mr. Shelden reached the draw where it was wide enough to turn out, he did so, but Hansen ran into him in such a manner as to overturn Mr. Shelden's carriage, throwing him out and starting his horses into a run. As they approached the Hancock end of the bridge one of his horses struck his leg against the stone abutment breaking it at the knee, throwing both down, injuring the other horse severely and making a wreck of the carriage. The horse that broke his leg was so badly injured that he had to be shot to put him out of his misery, the other horse is so badly injured that it is doubtful if he recovers. Hansen, the man who caused all the trouble, was arrested for cruelty to animals as it was found he had used a goad on his own horse in such a manner as to wound it severely. Hansen had a hearing before Justice Brand Tuesday, which was adjourned until today.

A hardened military man, George Shelden, appreciated good horse flesh. He was sickened by having to kill such a noble creature because of such a reckless, intentional act of viciousness. The carriage was easily replaced, but George had trouble stomaching why Hansen wantonly harmed the horses; and, God forbid, could have maimed him in the process.

While George was bruised and sore all over, he was giving his daughter away in marriage the following Tuesday and was glad he wasn't injured so badly that he couldn't do so. He shuddered to think that he could have been killed. He ruminated on why funerals and weddings were so intertwined, and why the first three letters in the word, funeral, spelled fun. His daughter was the apple of his eye, and he was proud of the woman she had become. Quickly, he turned his thoughts back to his schedule, totally unaware of the axiom that trouble, bad luck, and death come in threes--one from the devil, one from his wife, and one from their son.

Article 3
Copper Country Evening News
Vol IV Issue 271
Tuesday, September 29, 1896
Page 3

Portage Lake News

Miss Mary E. Shelden and Mr. B. T. Barry Wedded Today

Rev. J. E. Curzon Officiated.

Church Beautifully Decorated for the Occasion--Happy Couple Leave for Chicago

The marriage of Mary E., daughter of Mr. and Mrs. George C. Shelden, and Ben T. Barry, occurred this morning at 10:30 o'clock at Trinity church, in the presence of a large number of assembled friends and relatives. The impressive ceremony of the Episcopal church was read by Rev. J. E. Curzon.

The bride was attended by Miss Hubbell, as maid of honor, and Misses Nellie Gardner and Mary Edwards, as bridesmaids. The groom's best man was Mr. Lessing Karger, and Messrs. R. Skiff Shelden and Sam Karger acted as ushers. The bride was attired in white brocaded satin and chiffon, and the only ornament she wore was a large pearl crescent, the gift of the groom. She carried white roses. Miss Hubbell wore white organdy over white silk and carried maiden hair ferns. The bridesmaids wore white organdy over pale green and also carried maiden hair ferns. Mrs. Shelden, mother of the bride, was attired in heavy black silk trimmed with white lace, and the sister of the bride, Mrs. S. J. Bowling, wore her wedding gown of white silk and embroidered tulle.

The bride's gifts to her attendants were gold brooches set with pearls, while the groom presented his best man and ushers with diamond and pearl cravat pins.

The church was made beautiful for the happy event by decorations of white China asters with smilax and ferns. After the ceremony the wedding party was served with breakfast at the home of the bride's parents. The house and the table were beautifully decorated with pink and white China asters, carnations and smilax.

Mr. and Mrs. Barry left on the afternoon train for Chicago. They will also visit Jackson, Mich., the former home of Mr. Barry. They will return in about three weeks, when they will commence housekeeping in a home already prepared for their reception on Albion street, West Houghton.

Both the young people who start in life together under such auspicious circumstances have a host of friends in this community, who will wish them all happiness in their wedded life. The bride is a daughter of one of the oldest families in the county, and herself is a bright ornament in the society of the Portage Lake cities. Mr. Barry has been a resident of Houghton but five years, but in that time has become most popular by his genial ways and readiness to help along any object with his time and services. He is in business for himself and enjoys the good trade incident to continuing an old-established business.

The happiness of Mary's wedding day was only marred by the absence of her father. While there may have been much whispering in the pews, because George did not walk his daughter down the aisle and give her away; not one word was spoken out loud. Proper etiquette dictated that no one draw attention to his absence.

Mrs. Shelden shuddered to think that anyone outside the family would ever find out why George was absent. No word would escape her lips. George had been so badly beaten by his own coachman that he could barely stand without pain, much less walk their daughter down the aisle. If only there was a way to keep the story quiet.

Article 4
Portage Lake Mining Gazette
VOL XXXVIII., NO, 13.--WHOLE NO 1977
October 1, 1896
Page 3

WEDDING BELLS.

_____

"Happy is the bride the sun shines upon,"--if that be so then happy is the bride that became so in Trinity church last Tuesday morning--to the end did shine brightly when those solemn vows were taken, and the bride, we have reason to believe, will be one of the very happy ones if the judgment of her dearest friends be correct.

"What a delightful wedding!" was the unanimous exclamation of the crowd which emerged from Trinity church last Tuesday morning, after having witnessed the solemn service of marriage performed in a most impressive manner by the rector of the church, Rev. J. E. Curzon. The contracting parties, Miss M. E. Shelden and Mr. B. T. Barry, are well known and highly appreciated by a very large circle of friends who took great pleasure in being present at their nuptials.

The church was artistically yet simply decorated, for the occasion, with smilax, ferns and white daisies grouped in such a way that just the very best effect was produced.

Quite a while before the time mentioned for the ceremony arrived, the ushers, Messrs. R. Skiff Shelden and Samuel Karger were kept busy seating those who had been bidden to the marriage. Then as the hour drew near the immediate family and near relations came in and were seated in the front pews and Mrs. James P. Edwards took her seat at the organ--then everyone knew the time was drawing near, and there was almost a solemn hush throughout the church, though every head involuntarily turned, eager to catch the first glimpse of the bridal party which was heralded by the strains of music from the organ. The ushers leading the way were followed by the two bridesmaids tastefully dressed in white organdy over green silk and carrying bouquets of Maiden Hair--then came the Maid of Honor, Miss Florence Hubbell, dressed elegantly in white also carrying a bouquet of Maiden Hair--and then the bride charmingly attired in a white brocaded satin and bridal veil, holding in her hand a large bouquet of bridal roses and leaning on the arm of her brother-in-law, Mr. Bowling.

The party was met at the altar by the expectant groom and his best man, Mr. Leslie Karger. Having arranged themselves at the chancel, the rector in the beautiful service of the church pronounced those solemn words which bound them together for life, and they who had come into the church as twain went forth but one.

They left town on the noon train for a short trip, carrying with them the best wishes of hosts of friends.

At the depot a large number of people had gathered to say good-bye. Rice had been purchased by the bushel and was showered on them from all directions. The seats to be occupied by the bridal couple were trimmed with white ribbon, while on the outside of the car was a white placard bearing this inscription, "This is a bridal car."

★★★★★

I can envision the church filling up quickly as the ushers seated the guests. The fragrance of flowers wafting through the church is coupled with anticipation for the ceremony to begin. After the families are seated in the front pews, every head would turn to watch the procession as Mrs. Edwards at the organ thunderously begins the

Wedding March. The bridesmaids are exquisite in their organdy and satin gowns. Then, there is a hush, as everyone tries to catch their first glimpse of the bride. A vision of loveliness, Mary Shelden is radiant, as she slowly and majestically glides down the aisle on the arm of her brother-in-law, high color flushing her cheeks.

It must have been a wedding of which Cecile B. DeMille would have approved. No expense had been spared, and great attention had been paid to every detail. After the ceremony, a formal wedding breakfast was served at the magnificent Shelden home.

The ceremony had been perfect. Mary was overjoyed. She wanted her wedding day to last forever. She had cried so many tears, her handkerchief was sodden. While Mary's father hadn't been able to give her away, he was recovering well; and there was no need to worry. Glancing into the library, Mary had left open a book she loved by Kahlil Gibran. He had written that when joy is supping at your table, sorrow is asleep on your bed. Mary didn't think that Kahlil Gibran's quote held any meaning for her.

She was wrong.

Article 5
Copper Country Evening News
Vol IV Issue 274
Friday, October 2, 1896
Page 3

Portage Lake News

Mr. George C. Shelden Shot in Houghton

The Wounds Prove Fatal.

The deceased's Assailant supposed to Be Felix Dumonthier--He Jumps in the Lake.

George C. Shelden was shot on Houghton's main street last evening at 6:15, presumably by Felix Dumonthier. The shooting occurred across the street from Scott's laundry, near the Portage Lake bridge. The wounds inflicted were four in number. He died at 1:10 o'clock this morning.

Mr. Shelden was going home and was met by a man he afterward declared he was sure was Dumonthier. The latter grabbed him by the coat at the throat, asked him where he was going and immediately began to shoot.

Mr. Shelden fell to the sidewalk though he retained consciousness, when several people in the neighborhood, Dr. A. A. Anderson first, came running to the spot. He then and afterward declared that though it was dark he recognized Felix Dumonthier as his assailant.

No statement was signed by Mr. Shelden, before his death, but he told one of his friends that Felix came up in front of him and asked how he was going to settle the case and the deceased answered that he had already commenced the settlement before the justice, whereupon Mr. Shelden was conscious most of the time and that the physicians had hopes of his recovery until shortly before 1 o'clock, from which time he began to sink rapidly and died shortly after that hour.

From all accounts Dumonthier, as soon as he had done the shooting, ran to the bridge, out on it to the second span, climbed over the railing and jumped into the lake. The lake was dragged for several hours without any trace of the missing man being found. The officers visited his house and found he had not been there since the noon hour.

The wounded man was taken to his home, only a block and a half away, under the care of Dr. Jones, and Drs. Wheeler, Scallon, and Gassar were hastily summoned. They found the wounds to be four. One a scalp wound on the back of his head, one at the point of the jaw, which had fractured it, one in the upper part of one of the lower limbs and the waist, and one entering the neck on the left side and evidently running downward. The first three wounds, without the latter, would not be considered dangerous. At midnight the physicians reported the patient a little easier though their efforts so far had not located the bullet in the shoulder. At 1 o'clock, however, the change had come.

Although three or four persons saw a man running from the scene of the shooting and heard or saw the splash when he jumped from the bridge, yet there was considered to be doubt about whether the lake got the would-be murderer or not. None of those who saw any part of the occurrence recognized Dumonthier and the officers could find no one to absolutely say they saw him jump from the bridge.

Events of the past few days point to the Frenchman and supplied him with a motive. One night last week, Dumonthier or Felix, as he was familiarly called by everyone in Houghton, who was in Mr. Shelden's employ at the time, drove the latter to the Onigaming club house, where a dinner party was given. Felix was told to be at the club house at half-past ten and was there on time. After waiting some time he put the team in the shed and went into the kitchen of the house to keep warm. When Mr. Shelden came out he missed the man and finding him in the house began giving him a verbal shaking up which the Frenchman finally resented and out by the stables went for his employer in such a vigorous manner that Mr. Shelden since has been laid up from the effects.

Yesterday Felix was arrested on complaint of Mr. Shelden and his trial was to have come off today. It is supposed that crazed by his arrest and from brooding over the affair of last week, which caused it, he lay in wait to do the bloody deed he so well succeeded in and then threw himself off the bridge.

For an affair that happened on one of the principal streets, at so early an hour, there were a surprising number of conflicting rumors. The officers were kept busy looking up the different stories. After they had become satisfied that their man had really made way with himself they had to run down a story that Dumonthier had been seen in Hancock after the shooting.

News of the affair spread through the two towns like wildfire and the Houghton end of the bridge was alive with people in a very short time after the shooting. People lingered there until a late hour, talking over the tragedy and waiting for news from the Shelden house just up the hill. The lake was dragged until a late hour, but no trace of even a hat, or other garment, was found.

It now appears that a man named Bodette, who was crossing the bridge from Hancock, heard the shots and afterwards saw a man run along the bridge to about the second span and then climb over the railing and jump into the lake and afterward saw the body rise to the surface, but he did not recognize who it was; the water has been a depth of about twenty feet and the people are still dragging for the body. Felix had been working for Mr. Shelden for the last five years and leaves a wife and three children.

Mr. Carl Shelden was last evening attending a meeting in Marquette county and at its termination received the message informing him of the occurrence.

Mrs. Carl Shelden and daughter are in Chicago, but no doubt the whole party will return home tomorrow.

So far no pistol has been found, although it is reported one was seen on the ground after the shooting.

The deceased was born in Walworth county, Wisconsin, December 27, 1848, his parents being pioneer settlers of this county, and received a liberal education. Mr. Shelden during the rebellion was a member of Company D, Fourth Michigan Cavalry and was afterward made second lieutenant of Company D, of the Sixteenth Michigan Infantry; he afterward received a captain's commission. On leaving the regiment in 1865 he again became a resident of this county and purchased the brewery business in Hancock started by Mr. Peter Sauer. The brewery which stood where the Hancock depot now is was destroyed by fire in 1869. He afterward removed to Negaunee, where he started another brewery, but returned to Houghton in 1875.

Mr. Shelden was one of the promoters for building the Portage Lake bridge and the writer well remembers a trip to Bayfield with a party which Mr. Shelden joined at that place, his object in going there being to purchase long timbers for the bridge. After the bridge was completed the deceased acted, for many years, and until the bridge was sold to the county, as secretary and treasurer of the bridge company, but for the last few years he had been assisting in the management of his late father's estate.

Mr. Shelden was married to Miss Mary E. Edwards, one of the daughters of Capt. and Mrs. Edwards, also pioneer settlers of this district, April 17, 1867, by which marriage there were issue two children, Mrs. Bowling, of Detroit, who, with her husband, only left for Chicago on the afternoon of the day of the awful tragedy, and Mary E., who was last Tuesday married to Mr. B. T. Barry, and who left on this same day for Chicago, on their honeymoon, which has been brought to such an unhappy termination.

★★★★★

The commotion at the door, when George was carried into the house, brought Mary running into the foyer. She directed the men to carry George into the library where he was placed on their tufted fainting couch. As Mary stayed by her husband's side, she recalled when the Art Noveau movement began and how smitten she had been with the Louis Comfort Tiffany's lamps and the William Morris wallpapers. Morris said, "Have nothing in your houses which you do not know to be useful or believe to be beautiful." George had pored over the books of Morris' wallpapers with her, and they both had agreed upon the block print of dragonflies, fairies, and cabbage roses. They both thought it to be beautiful and appreciated his elegant decorative art style with the intricate patterns. The Tiffany glass and monochromatic wallpaper combined to create a peaceful haven in which to read and relax.

Georges Lemmen's Beach at Heist looked like a painting of Lake Superior with the light showcasing it. Even this night, the peaceful library helped ease the stress of the situation. The floor lamp gave off a kaleidoscope of lovely colors. George's condition seemed to be stabilizing until he beckoned for Mary to lean closer to him. He whispered, "Be strong my love, until we meet in Paradise." With that, George expired.

Mary was not to learn for weeks that William Morris had died the day after George.

Article 6
Copper Country Evening News
Vol IV Issue 275 (NOTE: Vol VI transposition error corrected here)
Saturday, October 3, 1896
Page 3

Portage Lake News

No Clue of George C. Shelden's Assailant Found

Still Searching the Lake

Funeral of the Murdered Man Has to Be Held Tomorrow Afternoon at 2 o'clock.

The authorities were busy all day yesterday seeking for Dumonthier's body and in the afternoon Sheriff Dunn procured some dynamite and tried to raise the body by that means, but the lake has so far not given up the dead.

The fact that Dumonthier was known to be an expert swimmer makes many persons believe that after he struck the water he swam ashore and is now in hiding. In case this should prove to be true, the sheriff has telegraphed a description of the man to the most likely points he would make for. However, from the statements of the Mr. Bodette, of whom the News spoke yesterday, it would appear most likely that the body is still in the lake. Mr. Bodette has not been very long from Canada and does not speak English, but the News reporter, by means of Mr. Bodette's brother, gathered that when on the draw, or just south of it, on his road to Houghton, he heard the pistol shots and shortly afterwards a man passed him very hurriedly and on looking back saw the person clamber over the rail (there are bloody finger marks on the rail) and jump into the lake. The man says that when the body struck the water it appeared to be doubled up and not as if a person, who was a swimmer, had dived; he saw the body rise and as he claims all was then quiet. It is most likely the body then sunk as it would be almost impossible for a person to swim ashore without Bodette, who was listening, hearing the ripple of the water.

The pistol is not, it appears, forthcoming; there was a rumor that a pistol was seen near the body, but as we understand it, such was not the case, at least if it was, the authorities report they have not been able to get hold of it; another report is that a boy saw a man running and as he was doing so he placed something in his pocket. This may have been the pistol and if the body is found it may so prove.

Mrs. Shelden was waiting supper for her husband and when Mr. George Quirk went to apprise her of the tragedy, she evidently had received some premonition, as she met him with the question, "Is it George or Felix?"

The funeral of Mr. Shelden will take place tomorrow (Sunday) afternoon at 2 o'clock and will be in charge of Houghton Lodge, F. & A. M., the members of which lodge and of the sister lodges are requested to meet at the Houghton lodge room at 2 o'clock sharp, in order to attend services.

Much commiseration is felt for Dumonthier's widow, if she is one, as well as for the Shelden family generally, as the sudden termination, and in such a manner, of a life which had such opportunities, must, indeed, be a sad blow to them.

★★★★★

Mary Shelden may have had a premonition that someone was to die. She thought that when the wedding and all the preparations were over, she would be able to settle down and relax. Instead, even though George had returned to work and appeared to have no long-lasting injuries, Mary was worried. Both of her daughters were safely and happily married, but a niggling sense of foreboding darkened Mary's world until it all turned black.

Neither George or Felix's wife could believe that she was a widow. While people came and went, only their mouths appeared to be moving. There was no connection between the words and the dreadful things that were coming out of their mouths.

Both women didn't believe that nightmares could happen when they were awake.

Article 7
L'Anse Sentinel
Vol XVI No 40
Saturday, October 3, 1896
Front Page

SHOT TO DEATH

Houghton Was the Scene of a Terrible Tragedy Thursday Evening.

GEO. C. SHELDEN THE VICTIM

Felix Dumonthier, the Murderer, then Ended His Own Life by Drowning.

Houghton was the scene of a shocking tragedy Thursday evening at 6:30 o'clock, whereby George C. Shelden, a prominent resident of that city, met an untimely death at the hands of his coachman, Felix Dumonthier. The particulars of the sad affair, according to report, are as follows:

Several days ago Mr. Shelden had some words with Dumonthier, who had been in his employ for several years as coachman, and the latter struck Mr. Shelden a severe blow. Later Mr. Shelden had the man arrested for assault and battery which resulted in his being fired. Thursday evening at the hour above stated, it is claimed that Dumonthier met Mr. Shelden near the Houghton end of the Portage Lake bridge, and asked him to pay the fine, which request was refused, whereupon Dumonthier drew a revolver and fired several shots at close range, each taking effect. Dumonthier then ran onto the bridge, and when about 100 feet from the shore jumped over the railing into the water, thirty-five feet below, and was drowned.

Mr. Shelden was at once taken to his home, only a block away from the scene of the shooting, and surgical attendance promptly secured. On examination it was found that his jaw was broken, one arm was paralyzed, a bullet had lodged in the brain and another had passed through his neck. Death resulted at 1 o'clock the following morning.

Deceased was 54 years of age, and was a brother of Carlos D. Shelden, the Republican nominee for congress from this district. He was a man well known throughout the upper peninsula, and had a host of friends who are greatly shocked at his tragic death.

Mr. Shelden's younger daughter was married Tuesday of this week and left for the east on her wedding tour. His elder daughter, Mrs. S. J. Bowling, left Thursday for her home in Detroit.

Dumonthier leaves a wife and five children. It was reported last evening that his body had not yet been recovered.

Article 8
Copper Country Evening News
Vol IV No 276
Monday, October 5, 1896
Page 3

Portage Lake News

Funeral of the Late G. C. Shelden Held Yesterday.

The Ontonagon Relief Fund.

The Northwestern Hotel to Go Under a New Management
Other Portage Lake News.

The funeral of George C. Shelden was held yesterday afternoon at 2 o'clock. It was very largely attended, there being friends of the family present, not only from Houghton and Hancock, but from the rest of the county and from the iron country. The services at the house were simple and were conducted by Rev. J. E. Curzon, of Trinity church. From the house to the cemetery and at the services at the grave, Houghton Lodge, F. & A. M., was in charge. The pall bearers were chosen to represent the Masonic order, the G. A. R. and the Loyal Legion, of all of which the deceased was a member. They were W. A. Dunn, J. N. Cox, Charles Smith, Dr. A. Wheeler, William Bath and H. B. Rogers.

The march to the grave was led by the Houghton Silver Cornet band, followed in order by Continental Hose Company, Company F, M. N. G., E. R. Stiles Post, G. A. R. Houghton Lodge, F. and A. M. and members of the other Masonic lodges. They followed the carriage containing the family and friends, the whole making a procession fully a mile and a half in length.

Article 9
Copper Country Evening News
Vol IV Issue 276
Wednesday, October 7, 1896
Page 3

Portage Lake News

————————

The Slayer of George Shelden Found Yesterday.

————————————

A Revolver With Five Exploded
Cartridges Found in His Pocket
   --Other News
A Bullet Wound in His Arm.

————————

The remains of Felix Dumonthier, the slayer of George Shelden, were recovered from Portage Lake yesterday afternoon shortly after 5 o'clock. The body was caught by the grappling hooks of one of the searching party that has been at work since Monday morning, when the finding of the hat convinced those interested that the lake had claimed the Frenchman.

The body was found within thirty feet of the first crib out from the Houghton shore, exactly where the telltale blood marks had indicated he had jumped.

All the dragging of the two days after the murder and the dynamite had apparently not touched the remains, which were in a good state of preservation. The dynamite too had been fired very close to the spot.

As the searchers were towing the body to shore the coat was pulled up over the head and from the hip pocket was immediately seen the fatal revolver. After being viewed by the coroner's jury the body was taken to Krellwitz's undertaking rooms and a careful examination was made.

A bullet wound was found in the left arm. The shot had gone through in a direction from the inside of the arm out, about two inches below the elbow.

The revolver found in Dumonthier's pocket was of 38 caliber. It is a five-shooter and the chamber contained five exploded cartridges. The finding of the body relieves the awful uncertainty of the poor wife and also assures her of the $2,000 life insurance which her husband carried in the Maccabee society. Mr. Dumonthier's funeral will take place tomorrow.

The finding of the pistol on Dumonthier's body would almost look as if there were two pistols in the affray as the young Hosking in his evidence at the coroner's inquest over Mr. Shelden yesterday afternoon and before Dumonthier's body was found, swore that he was the first to see Mr. Shelden after the shooting and at that time a pistol was lying by Mr. Shelden's shoulder. He stated that when Miss Morgan came over to see the body he told her to be careful as there was a pistol laying there. Miss Morgan in her evidence said that when she approached Mr. Shelden who was lying on the ground, she remembers that Hosking told her to be careful of something, but she could not remember what it was he referred to. Young Hosking, however, appeared positive it was a pistol he warned her against and explained minutely the position in which he said it was lying.

Article 10
Copper Country Evening News
Vol IV No 279
October 8, 1895
Page 3

Portage Lake News

––––––––––––––––

Inquest Over the Remains of Felix Dumonthier.

––––––––––––––––––––––––––––––––––

He Met Death By Drowning

––––––––––––––––––

While Laboring Under Great Mental Excitement Was the Verdict Returned

At the inquest over the remains of Felix Dumonthier, held yesterday before Justice Brand, the principal testimony, besides that relating particularly to the manner of the man's death, was regarding the bullet wound found in his left arm. This was given by Drs. Wheeler and Scott. The description of the wound was so given in yesterday's news and the principal thing about it, that the bullet passed through from the inside of the arm out, was established. It was such a wound as might have been inflicted on or by the dead man though its position was such as made the probability greater that the bullet came from Felix's own revolver.

Dr. Anderson, who arrived on the fatal scene almost as soon as the lad, Will Hosking, is just as certain that no revolver lay by Shelden as the boy is that he saw one there. Dr. Anderson says that the boy stood back evidently reluctant to approach the wounded man, while he himself went close to him and approached on the left side just where Hosking claims he saw the gun.

The jury in the Dumonthier inquest rendered a verdict that the deceased came to his death by drowning while laboring under great mental excitement.

Article 11
Portage Lake Mining Gazette
VOL XXXVIII., NO 14.--WHOLE NO 1978
October 8, 1896
Page 3

ABOUT PORTAGE LAKE.
_____

For the last week Houghton County, and Houghton in particular, where the sad affair occurred, has been much agitated; over the murder of George C. Shelden, suspicion pointing to Felix Dumonthier, a former coachman of the deceased. It seems about two weeks ago, Dumonthier was as he thought altogether too severely reprimanded by Mr. Shelden, and after standing it some time turned upon his employer and gave him a severe thrashing, so severe in fact that he was unable to leave the house for several days. Dumonthier was discharged and here the matter remained until last Thursday. Thursday Mr. Shelden had his former coachman arrested for assault and battery, the hearing being adjourned until Saturday. In the meantime the prisoner was liberated on bail. In the evening as Mr. Shelden was going home to supper he met his assailant, supposedly Dumonthier, on Shelden street just in front of the house occupied by Mr. and Mrs. Trebilcock. Mrs. Trebilcock in giving her testimony said that the two men came together. It was too dark for her to see who they were and after having a few words five shots were fired. Mr. Shelden was shot in four places, namely in the jaw, in the back of the head, in the neck and in the leg. After firing the last shot the assailant ran down the street out onto the bridge and jumped over the railing into the water. After being carried to his home Mr. Shelden declared before two witnesses that he was shot by Felix Dumonthier; this as yet is the only direct evidence that Dumonthier was the assailant. Of course in a matter of this kind there have been many senseless rumors afloat, but to fine everything down there seems to be little doubt but what Mr. Shelden was killed by Dumonthier who afterwards committed suicide by jumping into the lake and the best information we can obtain is that the latter could not swim. Monday morning a hat which has been identified as that of Dumonthier was found on the shore of the lake not far from the spot where he jumped from the bridge. A coroner's jury was summoned last Saturday, which after hearing what the following witnesses had to say adjourned until Tuesday. Mr. Trebilcock and wife, Dr. Wheeler, Dr. Anderson, Andrew Wier, Garist Rath, Louis Vontach and C. Brand. The funeral under the charge of Houghton Lodge F. & A. M., of which the deceased was a member, was held Sunday from his late residence, the remains being interred in Forest Hill cemetery.

Tuesday afternoon the coroner's jury again met when the following witnesses gave their testimony:

Miss Mary J. Morgan was the first witness called and testified that there was quite a pause between the first and second shots, the next three being in quick succession. She saw no struggle, but the three last shots were fired at Mr. Shelden while he was on the ground. The man that did the shooting was facing East and after firing the last shot walked away toward the bridge. Somebody asked Mr. Shelden who did it, Felix? And he replied yes, Felix. Mrs. Chas. Kohl heard the shooting while in the house. When she got out on the porch she saw a man run onto the bridge and shortly afterwards heard a splash. Wm. Hosking being called to the stand testified that he was the first person on the spot and that he saw a revolver lying by the side of Mr. Shelden, on the sidewalk, that he thought Miss Morgan was going to step on it and pulled her away. He was very positive that the revolver was there. Hosking was the one who went for Dr. Wheeler. When they returned to the spot the Dr. sent him for a rig; said it was some time between the first and second shots, last three shots being fired in quick succession. Hosking did not see the first shot but did see the last four fired. Harry Kohl was playing in the street near the scene of the murder and spoke to Mr. Shelden as he passed. He soon heard a shot fired and soon afterward four more. He ran to the spot and found it was Mr. Shelden. Edward Romph heard the shots and saw a man run out onto the bridge. He heard Dr. Wheeler ask Mr. Shelden who shot him, his reply being "Felix." Mr. Archy Mayotte of Hancock, said Felix came into his place late in the afternoon and seemed to be in good spirits. He wanted a lawyer and Mr. Mayotte promised to introduce him to Mr. Finnegan the next day. Felix drank a glass of pop and left at just about six o'clock. John Klingkammer was crossing the bridge and when near this end heard the shots fired, soon a man ran past him, could not tell who he was, saw him run about 200 feet and then lost sight of him. Frank Demaroe the last witness called said that he was on the opposite side of the street when the shooting took place, there being some time between the first and second shots. He looked toward the firing and saw one man holding another by the collar. After the third shot the man seemed to lay the man down on the walk, fire two more shots at him and then walk away carrying the pistol with him, when he lost sight of him. Witness was positive that the man carried the revolver away with him. At this point the jury adjourned until Saturday.

Tuesday afternoon at about five o'clock the body of Dumonthier was recovered, not far from the point where he was supposed to have jumped into the water. Upon examination he was found to have a pistol wound in his left arm about two inches below the elbow. In his coat pocket was found a 38 caliber, No. 9,479 Merwin Holbert & Co., self-cocking revolver together with five empty 38 caliber shells in the chambers of the revolver. There were no cartridges found on his person. His watch was also found. It was full of water and had stopped at 6:22 or 6:23. The adjourned coroner's jury met at Justice Brand's office yesterday morning. Dr. Scott being summoned said he had examined the body and found a bullet wound on the left forearm which had entered from the inside and passed out of the back of the arm. The flesh on the arm showed no scorching from powder; the bullet hole pointed backward and upward. The men who recovered the body say it was found about 30 feet west of the bridge.

August Krellwitz, the undertaker, testified that he found a revolver, some small change, some keys, and a watch on the deceased. He found a wound in the left arm just below the elbow. It was a clear bullet hole, taking an upward course and showing no sign of powder marks.

Archy Mayotte testified that he had known Felix Dumonthier for ten years and never knew him to carry a revolver. At six o'clock when he left his place the deceased was sober and showed no excitement.

Paul LaBelle testified that he was with the deceased for about an hour and a half, that he went into Mayotte's with him, that Felix talked on ordinary matters. Had known Felix for 7 or 8 years and never knew him to carry a revolver. That he thought he and Felix left Mayotte's at five or six minutes past six when he went to supper and Dumonthier left for Houghton, that when they parted Felix was perfectly sober and showed no excitement.

Z. Beauchamps testified that Felix was in his place, but he was unable to give any information of any interest. No more witnesses were summoned and the jury brought in the following verdict: We find that Felix Dumontheir came to his death, by drowning in Portage Lake. The drowning being his own act, while laboring under great excitement amounting to temporary insanity.

Embedded in the announcements, there were the following four lines:

The funeral of the late Felix Dumonthier was held this morning, the services being conducted by the K.O.T.M. of which he was a member.

There were 42 lines devoted to George Shelden.

OBITUARY

Mr. George C. Shelden was the son of the late Ransom and Theresa M. Shelden and was born in Walworth Co., Wis., December 27th, 1848. He was educated at Mount Clemens,
Ann Arbor and Ypsilanti, this state. In
September 1863, he enlisted as a private in
Company D, Fourth Regiment, Michigan
Cavalry and was transferred to Company D,
Sixteenth Michigan Infantry in the spring
1864, being commissioned Second Lieut. In April 1865, he was promoted to Captain and served until the close of the winter of 1865. Mr. Shelden was married April 17th,
1867 to Miss Mary E. Edwards, who with two daughters Mrs. S. J. Bowling, of Detroit and Mrs. B. T. Barry, of Houghton, survive him.

_____

Resolutions of Respect

_____

At a special meeting of Houghton
Lodge No. 218, F. & A. M. held October 4th the following resolutions were adopted:

WHEREAS In obedience to the mandate of our Supreme Grand Master, our worthy deceased brother, George C. Shelden, has been called to the Grand Lodge on High and it is befitting that Houghton Lodge No. 218 F. & A. M. should suitably record and express its sentiments in regard to our late brother,

Therefore be it

Resolved, That by his death it met with a loss which it deeply deplores. He was a lover of home, a devoted husband, a kind father and a generous citizen.

Resolved, That this lodge extend to the widow and family of the deceased in their great bereavement its sympathy and that the lodge be clothed in the emblem of mourning for the customary period, and these resolutions be recorded in the archives of this lodge and a copy be presented to the widow of the deceased and also a copy to the local newspaper with the request for publication.

M. R. Hoar
J. S. Penrose
Fred Stoyle

Articles 12-13
L'Anse Sentinel
Vol XVI No 41
Saturday, October 10, 1896
Front Page

George C. Shelden's Funeral.

All that was mortal of the late George C. Shelden was laid to rest Sunday afternoon. The funeral services, conducted by Rev. J. E. Curzon, were held at the family residence at 2 o'clock and were very impressive. During the services the procession had formed in the following order: Houghton Silver Cornet Band, Continental Fire Company No. 1, Houghton Light Infantry, E. R. Stiles post (G. A. R.) and F. & A. M. lodge No. 218. At the conclusion of the services the remains were borne by the pallbearers. Dr. A. M. Wheeler, Col. J. N. Cox, Sheriff W. A. Dunn, W. A. Bath, Horace Rogers and Hon. Charles Smith to the hearse and the march to Forest Hill cemetery began. The societies in line were followed by many carriages, the whole being about two miles in length, making it the largest funeral procession ever witnessed on Portage lake. The Masonic fraternity had charge of the funeral and at the grave the solemn and beautiful burial ritual of the order was read by William Bath.

The loss of Geo. C. Shelden to the town of which he has long been a prominent and patriotic citizen will be long felt in many a home which has been a recipient of his quiet generosity and charity. His great love of Houghton was doubtless attributable to the fact that his father was its founder, and its pioneer industries were all connected with the name of Ransom Shelden. There was no enterprise calculated to redound to the financial or social interests of his native village that did not receive the liberal support of George C. Shelden. His loss is a sad blow to Houghton, and his place in the community will be hard to fill.

The remains laid in state at the family residence Saturday, and up to the hour of the obsequies were visited by hundreds of friends and acquaintances of the deceased.--Mining Journal.

★★★★★

Mary dressed in black for heavy mourning accepted the condolences from family and friends. Both of her daughters were white-faced and still in shock. Poor, poor Mary!

Her honeymoon would never hold any happy memories for her or Ben. Jennie was sorry that they had left in the morning instead of leaving the following day. How she wished that they had stayed over an extra day! How she wished for even just a few more minutes with her father! Sam saw the sadness in his wife's eyes actually change her eye color.

The mourners came and went. There was an endless stream of people; until, finally, the interminable visitation was over.

Mary, George's widow, moved robot-like on Sunday. She made all the correct responses. Her behavior was befitting an imperious dowager. The enormity of the size of the procession and the pomp and circumstance made everything seem surreal.

George's funeral was the largest funeral ever held in the City of Houghton. The Silver Cornet Band led the procession to the cemetery and played the funeral dirges appropriate for such a solemn occasion. In the carriage, Mary wondered why the sun kept on shining when it was the end of her world. She remembered Emily Dickinson's poem:

Because I could not stop for death

He kindly stopped for me.

The carriage held but just ourselves and immortality.

As the carriage wheels kept turning and the band kept playing, Mary kept praying that she would just wake up; and the nightmare would be over.

When Reverend Curzon performed the graveside service, he noted that only a few days had passed since he had performed the wedding nuptials for other members of this same family. He pondered the vicissitudes of life, as he gave his eulogy. To the powerful, he gave his pomp.

When the family returned to the house, she kissed them all good night. Mary recalled Edgar Allen Poe's words: Leave my loneliness unbroken. Then instead of retiring, Mary climbed up to the tower and looked out the window as if to survey her sorrow. More of Edgar Allen Poe's words haunted her:

From a proud tower in the town,

Death looks gigantically down.

She descended woodenly to her second-floor bedroom, put on her night clothes, and got quickly into her side of the bed so as not to disturb George.

It was then that she started screaming.

A second article also appeared on the Front Page of the L'Anse Sentinel as follows:

DUMONTHIER'S BODY FOUND

Recovered From Portage Lake--There was a Bullet Wound in His Left Arm.

The remains of Felix Dumonthier, the slayer of George Shelden, were recovered from Portage Lake Tuesday afternoon shortly after 5 o'clock. The body was caught by the grappling hooks of one of the searching party that had been at work since Monday morning says the Calumet Evening News when the finding of the hat convinced those interested that the lake had claimed the Frenchman.

The body was found within thirty feet of the first crib out from the Houghton shore exactly where the telltale marks had indicated he had jumped.

All the dragging of the two days after the murder and the dynamite had apparently not touched the remains which were in good state of preservation. The dynamite too had been fired very close to the spot.

As the searchers were towing the body to shore the coat was pulled up over the head and from the hip pocket was immediately seen the fatal revolver. After being viewed by the coroner's jury, the body was taken to Krellwitz's undertaking rooms and a careful examination was made.

A bullet wound was found in the left arm. The shot had gone through in a direction from the inside of the arm out about two inches below the elbow.

The revolver found in Dumonthier's pocket was of 38 caliber. It is a five shooter and the chamber contained five exploded cartridges.

The finding of the pistol on Dumonthier's body would almost look as if there were two pistols in the affray, as young Hosking in his evidence at the coroner's inquest over Mr. Shelden Tuesday afternoon and before Dumonthier's body was found, swore that he was the first to see Mr. Shelden after the shooting and at that time a pistol was lying by Mr. Shelden's shoulder. He stated that when Miss Morgan came over to see the body he told her to be careful as there was a pistol laying there. Miss Morgan in her evidence said that when she approached Mr. Shelden who was lying on the ground, she remembers that Hosking told her to be careful of something, but she could not remember what he referred to. Young Hosking, however, appeared positive it was a pistol he warned her against and explained minutely the position in which he said it was lying.

The funeral was held from the residence yesterday morning at 10 o'clock. Deceased was a member of the Maccabee society, and carried a policy of $2,000.

★★★★★

Can you imagine dynamiting the lake in an effort to recover a body? I would think that just the opposite could happen. It is befuddling to me, and a miracle that they didn't blow Felix Dumonthier to bits with such a drastic method of recovery.

Article 14
Copper Country Evening News
Vol IV Issue 282
Monday, October, 12, 1896
Page 4

The Shelden Inquest

The coroner's inquest was brought to a termination on Saturday afternoon by the return of the following verdict:

'The deceased came to his death by reason of a wound from a revolver in the hands of Felix Dumonthier while the latter was temporarily insane.'

This must take a great weight off the minds of the living members of the two families mixed up in the most lamentable affair, and will also, it is to be hoped, prove a lesson to the community at large.

Now that you have read the accounts in the newspapers of the day, you have all the information I was able to locate. I was unable to find death certificates or inquest records at either the Houghton County Courthouse or the Michigan Tech Archives.

The news articles were presented first to provide a chronological paper trail in the order in which the events unfolded to the public. I am including an article I wrote for the Daily Mining Gazette. It is an abridged account of these events. I gave one-time permission to the newspaper to run it, because I believed that Bridgefest should include a bridge story every year.

I gave the receptionist a printed copy of the story. She asked if I had a disk copy. I told her that no one had even suggested I give them my story on disk and did not have the time to drive 11 miles each way to get the disk prior to my luncheon engagement. Another woman said that someone there would retype it. I left with misgivings, but I had done precisely what I had agreed to do.

After lunch, since I take great pride in my work, I asked my cousin, Barbara Herres, if we could stop back at the newspaper to see if the staff had any problems with my story. When I queried if the article was typed as submitted, the receptionist told me in no uncertain terms, "It was typed exactly as you gave it to us." The emphasis on exactly left no room for me to question its final form. We left, and since Barb gets her paper hours before I do; I asked her to call me the next day when the article was to appear and read it to me. She told me that it looked great, and that they had added a photograph of the bridge which enhanced the article. Then she started reading it to me. She began to laugh, and by the ninth error could hardly stop laughing.

One error was just dreadful. The article said that **Mr. Hosking testified that he was a revolver** laying by the side of Mr. Shelden won the sidewalk. Another witness who was across the street **was one man lay** the other man down and walked away carrying the pistol with him. It was heartbreaking as this is a jewel of a story, and my name was attached to it. I still feel sick about it, but Barb always apologizes for laughing. She was laughing, because the paper had really made a mess of my story. She never could have imagined three errors in two sentences. With spell check and grammar check on computers now, combined with proofreading, I find it inexcusable that these errors were not caught. When things are really grim, our family has the saving grace of laughter though. Now just to lighten heavy moments, we segue into "and Mr. Hosking testified that he was a revolver." If he had actually said that, wouldn't the coroner's jury have had a good laugh, too!

I am retelling this to serve as a reminder to you that you should **always trust your inner voice,** and even when others are adamant that everything is correct, check for yourself if you have that niggling feeling that something may be amiss, particularly when your name and reputation is attached to the work. Also, I wonder if I had requested payment for the story, if it would have been treated as more valuable. I just wanted to contribute to the Bridgefest festivities in my own small way.

I have never read the Gazette story in print. I am not sure of the total number of errors, but as Barb read it to me, we counted up to nine; and then I couldn't bear to read it for myself. I did put their newspaper clipping in my personal file, but I only read the headline and looked at the bridge photo. For those of you who would like to read the story fraught with errors, it appeared in the Daily MIning Gazette on Wednesday, June 11, 2008, page 7A.

I am happy to report that now I laugh that the newspaper printed that Mr. Hosking testified that he was a revolver. . . albeit, it still makes me sad. I worked hard on this story and thought I would be proud of it, instead I still feel shame and would appreciate anyone reading this to not look up this story as it appeared in the Daily Mining Gazette.

Here is the abridged bridge story which I submitted to the paper:

Every year Bridgefest brings the twin cities and the outlying communities together for a weekend of fun, food, and festivities.

Since this is Bridgefest, I can think of no better time to tell you a story about the bridge. I hope it piques your interest in the bridge and the pioneers who settled the Copper Country. This story is about one of the most prominent families in the area. It is the story of the George C. Shelden family. This is their bridge story; a tale of murder, marriage, and mayhem.

George Shelden's father, Ransom Shelden, married Theresa Houghton, and together, Ransom and Douglass came to Portage Entry and started mining, mercantile, and fishing businesses. They bought over 55,000 acres of land and platted the village of Houghton. Every enterprise they touched turned into copper.

George was born on December 27, 1842 and grew up a member of the noveau riche, living in a fine home, servants to cater to his every wish, and a coveted circle of friends and relatives. Their sphere of influence in the Copper Country made it possible for George to enter the rarefied world of successful men by virtue of birth. He had every advantage possible. His father's affiliation with the Republican party ensured that his other son, Carlos, became a Congressman, and George was instilled with an obligation to duty serving in the Civil War. He enlisted as a private, was commissioned Second Lieutenant, and finally promoted to Captain. Even though he was born with a silver spoon in his mouth, he proved himself worthy by his own actions.

After the war, George married Mary Edwards on April 17, 1867. Their marriage was blessed with two lovely daughters, Jennie and Mary. George was never happier than when he was in his home surrounded by the three women he loved.

Kahlil Gibran wrote that when joy is supping at your table, sorrow is asleep on your bed. Thus, it was true that when the Shelden family gathered for the happiest of family occasions, that sorrow was about to end their idyllic life. Jennie was already a married woman, Mrs. Bowling, and lived in Detroit with her husband. Mary, her sister, the baby of the family, was planning a fall wedding. All three women were consumed with planning the wedding of the century. George's wife, the mother of the bride, Jenny, the maid of honor, and Mary, the bride, spent the summer with such attention to detail that Cecil B. DeMille would have approved. Mary Shelden was to wed Mr. Barry in late September at the Trinity Church on the southwest corner of Pewabic and Montezuma Street in Houghton.

One evening about two weeks before Mary's wedding, George had dinner with some friends at the Onigaming Club, a private club at the time. George's coachman was to pick him up at 10:30 p.m., but kept George waiting. George severely reprimanded the coachman until outraged the coachman turned on his employer and gave him a severe thrashing, so severe that he couldn't walk his daughter down the aisle or leave his home for several days.

Mr. Shelden fired his coachman and had him arrested for assault and battery. The coachman was released on bail and a hearing was set for Saturday.

Recovering from his thrashing, George was regaled with every detail of his daughter's wedding, since he could not be in attendance. His wife, Mary, described the church as being decorated with smilax, ferns, and white daisies, simply but artistically. The guests all were from families associated with the most affluent residents in the Copper Country. The ushers were Skiff Shelden and Sam Karger. The organist was Mrs. James Edwards. George watched his wife's face glow as she relived the ceremony. The ushers leading the way were followed by the two bridesmaids tastefully dressed in white organdy over green silk and carrying bouquets of maiden hair. Then came the maid of honor, Miss Florence Hubbell, dressed elegantly in white also carrying a bouquet of maiden hair. Then came the bride charmingly attired in a white brocaded satin and bridal veil, holding in her hand a large bouquet of bridal roses and leaning on the arm of her brother-in-law, Mr. Bowling.

Mary continued giving her husband more details. The party was met at the altar by the groom and his best man, Leslie Karger. Reverend John Curzon conducted a beautiful ceremony, and the couple left on the noon train. At the Houghton depot rice was purchased by the barrel and showered on the newlyweds who left with the well wishes of their family and friends in a private car. On the outside of the car was a white placard: Wedding Car.

Mary's sister and brother-in-law left early on Thursday morning. The wedding couple had left for Chicago right after the ceremony Tuesday. I am sure that George's wife must have been ready to collapse like a broken doll.

She had been so busy planning a wedding, attending the wedding without her husband, handling all the details of the wedding, and adding to that the new additional worry over her husband's injuries. She wished that she could be in two places at once, at her husband's side and at her daughter's wedding.

Finally her husband went back to work, the wedding was proclaimed a success, and Thursday night was to be the first evening there would be no houseguests. Mary was exhausted and ready to retire early.

As George walked home, there were reports that his coachman met him and grabbed him by his topcoat in front of the Trebilcock home. Five shots rang out, and George fell to the sidewalk, mortally wounded. A man was seen running from the scene, a splash was heard, and it was believed that the man jumped to his own death.

The news spread like wildfire through the twin cities. George was carried to his home, and three physicians were in attendance. George had been hit by four shots. The first resulted in a scalp wound in the back of the head, the second one fractured his jaw, the third hit him in one of the upper lower limbs and the waist, but it was the fourth wound that was the most serious. The fourth bullet entered the neck on the left side and ran downward. By midnight the physicians were hopeful that George would recover; but at 1:00 a.m., George took a turn for the worst. The fourth injury proved to be fatal.

Most of the time, he had remained conscious, and though he did not sign a written statement, George told one of his friends that his coachman had come up to him and asked how he was going to settle the case and the deceased answered that he had already commenced the settlement before the justice, whereupon the shots were fired.

It was believed that the coachman ran onto the bridge, and when about 100 feet from the shore jumped over the railing into the water 35 feet below and was drowned. The lake was dragged and not even a hat was retrieved. Since no one actually saw the coachman shoot George Shelden or jump from the bridge, the police were kept busy investigating the stories, including an account of a sighting of the coachman later that evening in Hancock.

Because George Shelden named the coachman as his assailant, and because the coachman had motive, it was commonly believed that the coachman shot his former employer and then committed suicide by jumping off the bridge when he did not know how to swim.

There is a subtle irony in that George Shelden visited Bayfield and helped build the bridge here, even selling the lumber with which to build it and serving as Secretary and Treasurer until the bridge was sold to the county.

A coroner's jury was convened. Mary Morgan testified that there was quite a pause between the first and second shots, the next three being in quick succession. She saw no struggle but the three shots were fired when Mr. Shelden was on the ground. She then watched the coachman walk away and heard a splash. Mr. Hosking testified that he saw a revolver lying by the side of Mr. Shelden on the sidewalk. Another witness who was across the street saw one man lay the other one down and walk away carrying the pistol with him.

On October 6, 1896, Tuesday evening, a week after the wedding, the grappling hooks of the search party recovered the coachman's body. His hat had been recovered the day before. His watch was full of water and had stopped at 6:23 p.m. A 38-calibre revolver was found in his pocket. There was a bullet wound in the left arm from the inside of the arm out, about two inches below the elbow. The jury rendered a verdict that the coachman came to his death by drowning while laboring under great mental excitement.

Is this story a case of good versus evil? Is it another great American epic filled with didactic imagery? Which man is the villain? Which man is the victim? Is there a reason danger contains the word, anger? Were there two guns? And when you cross the bridge do you sometimes hear the cries of both men's families mingling with the howl of the north wind?

This article is excerpted from Unsolved Mysteries of the Copper Country: No. 2 The Case of George C. Shelden.

Permission for a one-time publication has been given to The Daily Mining Gazette for Bridgefest, 2008.

Other works by P. Germain include Tinsel & Tears, Lest We Forget, Copper Country Trivia, Thanks a Million, False Alarm, and Unsolved Mysteries of the Copper Country: No. 1: The Case of Hilda C. Johnson.

NOTE: The present bridge is the third bridge. The first bridge was located 135 feet from the present one.

Breakdown of Events by Date

Sept. 11	Suicide of Ira J. Whitney
Sept. 21	Accident on the Bridge
Sept. 21*	Beating of George Shelden by Felix Dumonthier
Sept. 29	Wedding of Mary Shelden and Ben Barry; couple leaves on train for honeymoon
October 1	George Shelden shot on Shelden Avenue
	Older daughter and husband leave town to return to downstate home
	Felix Dumonthier Missing
October 2	George Shelden Dies
October 3	George C. Shelden's remains lie in state at family residence
October 4	Funeral Procession and Funeral for George C. Shelden
October 6	Felix Dumonthier's Body Recovered
October 7	Felix Dumonthier's Inquest Verdict
October 8	Funeral for Felix Dumonthier
October 10	George C. Shelden's Inquest Verdict

---

* Date is an approximation.

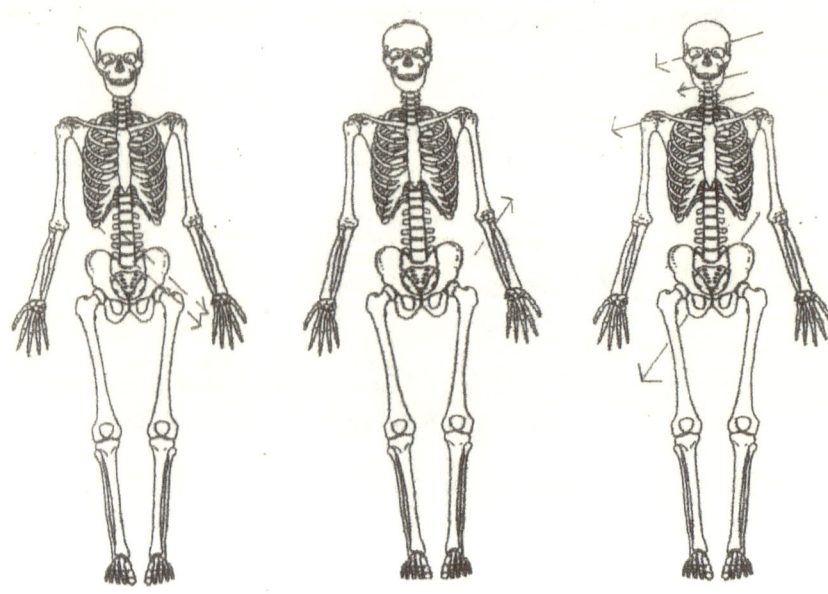

Ira J. Whitby	Felix Dumonthier	George Shelden
one shot right ear	shot in left arm from inside of the arm out	scalp wound back of head
two shots two inches below elbow		fractured jaw
		shot in neck on left side running downward
		shot in upper part of one of the lower limbs and waist*

Homunculi credit: Heather Harris, Joint POW/MIA Accounting Command Historian.

If a person is shot at close range, there is powder residue which can be washed off. Ira Whitby should have had some residue on his clothing.

If a person is shot from a few feet, there is stippling which does not wash away and is embedded in the skin. Was the distance ever calibrated to see how far apart Felix Dumonthier and George Shelden were at the time of the shooting? Were the casings in the gun found

---

* There is no specific citation of which lower limb the shot entered. The author believes it may have been the left thigh, but has no support documentation or empirical evidence to support this hypothesis.

in Felix Dumonthier's pocket examined to check if all five bullets had been fired?

Were all the men right-handers? How thorough were the investigations and subsequent inquests?

For those of you who wonder as I did if George Shelden had left a will and to whom he left his worldly goods, I telephoned the Houghton County Courthouse to see if there was a will on record. There is a $20 fee to find out whether or not a person has a will on file. If the answer is affirmative, then an individual may pay $1 per page to get a copy of it. For $23, I was able to get a copy of George Shelden's will. The pages were in shades varying from grey to black, almost indecipherable, and not straight on the page. I received eight pages, since the document was not printed on legal size. It is paraphrased below.

The first paragraph is as follows: In the name of God, Amen. I, George Shelden of Houghton, Houghton County and State of Michigan being of sound and disposing mind and memory calling to mind the frailty and uncertainty of human life and being desirous of settling my worldly affairs and directing the estate with which it has pleased God to bless me shall be disposed of after my decease, while I have the strength and capacity so to do, do make and publish this my last will and testament. And first I commend my immortal being to Him who gave it, and my body to earth to be buried by my executor hereinafter named. And as to my worldly estate and all the property real, personal, or mixed, of which I shall die seized and possessed, or to which I shall be entitled at the time of my decease, I devise, bequeath, and dispose thereof in the manner following, to wit:

After directing that all his just debts and funeral charges shall be paid by his executor, he gave, devised, and bequeathed to his beloved grandchildren, Fayette, Emmett, and Ella, the children and heirs of Timothy Shelden, all of his estate, both real, personal or mixed. He appointed his son, Ransom, as the executor. The will was dated June 22, 1869.

On May 9, 1871, George added a codicil that Ella's share should be invested and paid to her when she reached the aged of 21, together with the accumulated interest and profits. He also directed the terms of Fayette's bequest. That George Shelden lived 25 years after he had attached the codicil to his will insured that his grandchildren were no longer minor children. His brother, Carlos, was one of the witness of the will, and John Chassell was one of the witnesses of the codicil. There was never a mention of George having a son, Ransom, except in the will which in his own hand, George wrote: . . . I do nominate and appoint my son Ransom Shelden to be the executor of this my last will and testament.

When I visit my family plot at Forest Hill Cemetery in Houghton, I often take an immediate left as I go through the cemetery gates. The road curves to the right and skirts the edge of the perimeter of the cemetery. Just before you see the Hoar mausoleum, you will see a site on the left with a tall obelisk in the center with the name of Ransom Shelden, one of the area's most prominent founding fathers. This burial ground is gated. This is the Shelden Cemetery, a private cemetery for a family who led public lives.

Photo credit: Germain Private Archives.

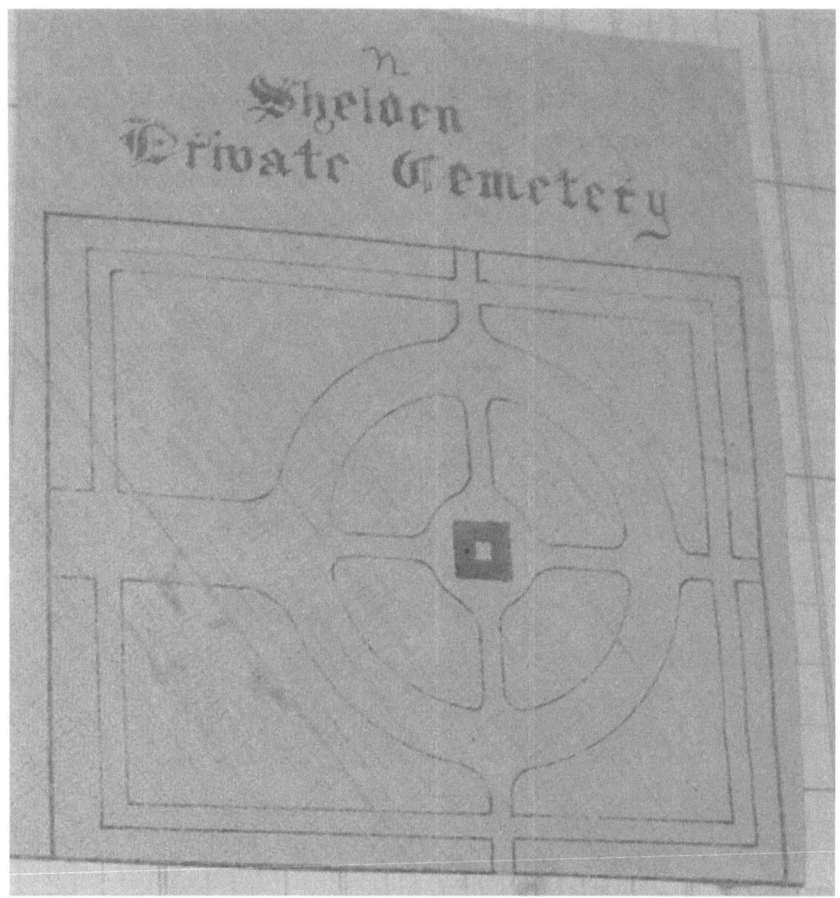

Photo credit: Germain Private Archives.

Every time I pass the Shelden plot, I always think that they must not have believed that they were going to be dead when they were at their cemetery, because the site is breathtakingly beautiful up high overlooking the twin cities of Houghton and Hancock. The circle drive with the wide expanse of footstones encircling the lot evokes a sense of grandeur with its private gate. The trees have grown up now, but I am sure that when the Sheldens bought this plot as their own private cemetery, they chose the finest lot available. Back then the trees were little saplings and didn't obstruct the view of the twin towns either. It must have been one of the finest building sites in the Copper Country. The Shelden Private Cemetery has an elegant, well-designed layout befitting this wealthy, distinguished, aristocratic family that sleeps in death on this grassy knoll.

It is a setting that befits a park, and I would have enjoyed savoring a picnic luncheon if I was the owner, and still may since the gate is not locked. The last time I visited the Sheldens, I brought a new flag to George for his military service, compliments of VFW Post #3900, Commander Dan Caron.

Photo credit: Germain Private Archives.

The Sheldens traveled in a rarefied social circle, and even in death remain aloof from the masses by the private gate which separates the Shelden Private Cemetery from the abutting Forest Hill Cemetery.

The Shelden Private Cemetery is not a plot inside the boundaries of the Forest Hill Cemetery, as I originally believed. The sexton of the Forest Hill Cemetery, Martin Heikkila, explained that the Forest Hill Cemetery staff maintains the Shelden Private Cemetery.

On the tax record which I got at the Houghton County Equalization Department, Portage Township is the owner of record. Both of the individuals I spoke with at the township directed me to call the City of Houghton, because when I read them the tax number, starting with 052, I was told that it is a City of Houghton number. I was admonished that I shouldn't have called the Portage Township Offices.

The woman I spoke with at the City of Houghton remarked that it was strange. Clearly, if the number begins with 052, it should be a property in the City of Houghton. Since the owner of record listed is the Portage Township Offices and includes the address for the township offices, the 052 number should be corrected.

It is also notable that cemeteries do not have to pay taxes.

Now that you have read the text and assimilated the information, you may wish to decide what the truth is. I have included a few scenarios to stimulate your own hypotheses and arrive at your own conclusions. The truth doesn't change--even after 100 years!

In reading and rereading the articles, there are inconsistencies. Did Felix Dumonthier have a wife and three children or a wife and five children? Was he an expert swimmer or could he not swim? Did he commit suicide by jumping off the bridge, or did he drown because he had a gunshot wound right below his elbow which rendered the arm useless?

Did the coroner's verdict list drowning instead of suicide so that Felix's widow and children would be able to collect on the $2,000 insurance policy he carried?

Was George Shelden shot in the jaw, leg, back of head, and neck; or was he shot in the jaw, upper leg and waist, back of head, and arm? Why was one shot fired, and then a pause before another shot followed by three more shots? Did one man fire the first shot and then a second; and the second man shoot back three times? How thoroughly was the evidence examined and analyzed before the coroner's jury rendered a verdict?

How many children did each man sire? Because George Shelden appointed his son, Ransom, as his executor, why was there no mention of any other children in addition to Jennie and Mary prior to the appointment of George's son as George's executor? Could George have meant to appoint his nephew, R. Skiff, Ransom Skiff that is, and written son instead of nephew by mistake? It is unclear how many sons and daughters were of George's issue, since Timothy's children were George's beloved grandchildren.

Scenario One

George Shelden had every right to expect the coachman to be waiting for him

Provoked by having to wait, George was justified in upbraiding his coachman for being so lax. The hot-tempered coachman had been deservedly fired and arrested for assault and battery.

Felix Dumonthier, while released from jail until his trial, couldn't provide for his family if George Shelden didn't give him back his job. Felix approached George on the street to plead for his job and in the heat of anger, shot his employer to death when George smugly told him he wouldn't give him his job back. The haughty Mr. Shelden met his employee's pleas to come back to work with disdain. He acted as if he were simply brushing a fly off his lapel, and turned away from Felix to end the conversation. The hot-blooded and equally hot-headed Frenchman did not even realize that the gun was being fired and was equally shocked that it was his very own hand that was doing so.

Felix in a fit of rage, killed his employer, George Shelden; and then jumped off the bridge to end his own life when he realized what he had done. If only Felix's bad temper hadn't gotten the better of him. Twice.

Scenario Two

Having been thrashed by Felix Dumonthier, his coachman, and laid up from the injuries, George Shelden filed charges against the man and fired him from his job. When George Shelden saw his coachman approaching him on the street a few days before the court hearing, frightened, he removed the pistol from his own pocket as soon as he recognized who was coming toward him. George wanted to ward off his former coachman, not knowing that the man was only there to plead for his job. George fired his pistol before a word was spoken. Wounded in the left forearm, Felix Dumonthier, feared for his own life, and returned gunfire. Then, realizing that George was mortally wounded, the coachman ran away.

As Felix Dumonthier ran toward the bridge, he knew that he wouldn't stand a chance of a fair trial. His employer had powerful friends in the court system. Their lies would become the truth. No one would believe that his employer had shot first and that he had only fired his gun in self-defense. Felix jumped off the bridge to his own death rather than stand trial. As the water closed over his head, he wondered how it had all gone so wrong for him . His last prayer was that his wife and family would believe that he had acted in self-defense and that the new baby would be healthy.

Scenario Three

George Shelden brought his own death upon himself. He should never have berated his coachman for being in the kitchen trying to warm his hands and feet when he found him. If George had been ready to leave the Onigaming at the designated time he had requested to be driven home, Felix would have been waiting for him. Only after such a long wait on such a cold evening, did the coachman go inside for a few minutes to warm up.

George wouldn't even give Felix a chance to explain. After berating the coachman for several minutes, the coachman was justified in beating his arrogant employer. If George was reasonable, he would have fought back like a man; and they could have both taken a few licks and settled the score. Instead, George got Felix arrested and fired him on the spot.

George Shelden always had to win, and he deserved to die like an animal in the streets for his arrogance.

Scenario Four

George had many business enterprises. Because he was such an astute businessman, often he realized large profits when men with less business acumen were suffering terrible losses. To George, business was just business. Sometimes there were gains; sometimes there were losses. As his fortune grew, he became even more successful as he took larger risks. It never occurred to George that a man who suffered losses would try to harm him simply because he was a better businessman.

George would have found it preposterous that a man he had bested in business would actually hire someone else to have George harmed. The accident on the bridge appeared to have nothing to do with anyone with whom George had done business.

When the accident didn't harm George, George's business rival decided to murder the man who had destroyed his business. He got his chance on the night of October 1, 1896. The only guilt he felt was that an innocent man got blamed for his crime.

As a believer in historic integrity and thorough documentation, the George C. Shelden story has too many loose ends to definitively prove or disprove that whichever scenario you chose is not the correct one. You may prefer to develop a conspiracy theory or believe that there may even have been a deadly love triangle.

Do trouble, bad luck, and death travel together? If George Shelden knew that in the Fall of 1896, there would be three dead men, three widows, three funerals, and three inquests, would he have run a matchstick under running water? Would George have admitted that he, too, had a gun, so that there would also have been three guns? Did the three doctors who attended him hide his gun?

I couldn't locate the death certificates. I couldn't locate the coroner's inquest testimony. I couldn't locate the fine Shelden home. I couldn't locate the murder weapon.

What I could do--and did do--is bring the story to your attention.

Let George Shelden's story stand as a tribute to his contributions to the Copper Country of the past!

The Shelden Block, the building which George dreamed would stand on the corner of Isle Royale Street and Shelden Avenue, became a reality. George's wife, Mary, did not let George's dream die with him. The Shelden Block was completed by the end of the century at a cost of $75,000, and was built of the locally quarried red sandstone that George favored.

Photo credit: MTU Archives and Copper Country Historical Collections, Michigan Technological University.

A century after its completion, the Shelden Block, still stands on the northwest corner of Shelden Avenue and Isle Royale Street.

Photo credit: Germain Private Archives.

Note the detailing and fine craftsmanship of the sandstone arches above the doors.

Photo credit: Germain Private Archives.

John Dee partnered with George's widow, Mary, so that they both had twin halves with store fronts on the street level and offices on the upper two stories. The Shelden half was the half on the corner. George and Mary's son-in-law, Ben Barry, ran the B. T. Barry drug store, on the main street level; and R. Skiff Shelden, their nephew, had his law practice upstairs. As a tribute to her husband, Mary had the Shelden name grouted into the tile of the vestibule going to the offices upstairs.

The upstairs houses apartments now, and the vestibule is kept locked. When I peered through the glass of the doors, I caught my breath when I discovered the Shelden name in the tile work. This photograph continues to elicit the magic of that moment when I saw their name for the first time.

Having to take the photograph from outside the building and through the glass of the doors was also reminiscent of the Shelden family's desire for privacy and need for one to have an invitation to enter their world.

Photo credit: Germain Private Archives.

Because even a simple man is complex, I find it difficult to move quickly through a graveyard. I want to know all of the stories of the people that lived and died here. That is why I now present to you vignettes of two others who are in the Shelden Private Cemetery.

The dead do not see the destiny of their descendants nor do they know what trials and tribulations have befallen their relatives and friends since their own passing. I am sure that George Shelden would have been saddened to learn that his nephew, R. Skiff Shelden, his brother Carlos's son, died in the prime of his life also. He would have been proud of how R. Skiff had handled the family's finances, but shocked that another happy time was turned into a tragedy for his family.

The Daily Mining Gazette reported that Ransom Skiff Shelden died in Nice, France at the age of 53 on March 27, 1922. He and three traveling companions took a Grand Tour, one of Frank C. Clark's world tours. The trip included stops in Egypt, Greece, and Italy. The group was on their way homeward when Skiff caught pneumonia and died.

His three traveling companions survived.

Photo credit: Germain Private Archives.

Another occupant of the Shelden Private Cemetery is Rev. Cowley-Carroll. Because the Sheldens were staunch Episcopalians, George would have embraced the invitation to have a priest from his Trinity Episcopalian Church be buried with the family, but he would have been as profoundly shocked as the community to learn that the Rev. Hubert Cowley-Carroll was found dead in his garage as reported in the Daily Mining Gazette on October 26, 1933.

The doors of the garage may have blown shut while he was busily repairing his car. He had a screwdriver in his right hand, and there were tools on the floor. The ignition was on and the gas tank was empty. Death was caused by carbon monoxide poisoning.

George C. Shelden, his nephew, R. Skiff Shelden, and the priest, Rev. Cowley-Carroll each of these three men died within months of his own 54th birthday.

Photo credit: Germain Private Archives.

Abraham Lincoln believed man's greatest invention was the written word. It allows one to talk to the absent, the dead, and the yet unborn. I agree.

Thank you for viewing the past through my window of words!

Bibliography

Homunculi

Blank Homunculi: Heather Harris, Joint POW/MIA Accounting Command Historian, Hickam Air Force Base, HI.

Newspapers

Copper Country Evening News: Articles 3-5-6-8-9-10-14. Microfilm Collection, MTU Archives & Copper Country Historical Collections, Michigan Technological University, Michigan.

Germain, P. June 11, 2008. Daily Mining Gazette, Tale of murder, marriage and mayhem A bridge story about the George C. Shelden family, Page 7A, Houghton, MI.

L'Anse Sentinel: Articles 7-12-13. Microfilm Collection, MTU Archives & Copper Country Historical Collections, Michigan Technological University, Michigan.

Portage Lake Mining Gazette: Articles 1-2-4-11. Microfilm Collection, MTU Archives & Copper Country Historical Collections, Michigan Technological University, Michigan.

Public Documents

Last Will and Testament of George C. Shelden dated May 11, 1896, Houghton County Courthouse, Houghton, MI.

Photographs

Germain Private Archives, Calumet, MI.

Photograph No. MTU Neg 00337, "G. C. Shelden Mansion with ornate porch and swing," Date unknown. Roy Drier Photographic

Collection. MTU Archives and Copper Country Historical Collections, Michigan Technological University, Michigan.

Photograph No. MTU Neg 00406, "Shelden Block, Houghton," Date unknown. Roy Drier Photographic Collection. MTU Archives and Copper Country Historical Collections, Michigan Technological University, Michigan.

Maps

City of Houghton, U. P. Engineers & Architects, Inc., 100 Portage Street, Houghton, MI 49931.

Shelden Private Cemetery/Forest Hill Cemetery, Martin Heikkila, sexton.

About the Author

P. Germain, a fourth-generation member of Calumet's early settlers, is oft quoted as saying, "I live in Calumet because people know what you are doing, but in Lake Linden they know what you are thinking."

Life confined to a small geographic area is a microcosm of a larger area. The people and events are more intricately entwined, because everyone knows each other. Here people do not have their noses in your business, they have their hearts in each other's troubles.

Fascinated with people, the author received an Associate in Commerce degree, a Bachelor's degree in Business Education, and a Master's degree in Guidance and Counseling. Equally fascinated with buildings, the author also has a broker's license in real estate.

P. Germain has taught at both the high school and college levels, listed and sold real estate, and published several local history works. Earlier works include Tinsel & Tears, False Alarm, Copper Country Trivia, Lest We Forget, and Thanks a Million.

www.ingramcontent.com/pod-product-compliance
Lightning Source LLC
Chambersburg PA
CBHW021241280526
45784CB00005B/2185